OSVALDO GOLIJOV

FISH TALE

FOR FLUTE AND GUITAR

ISBN 978-1-4950-7891-0

HENDON MUSIC

BOOSEY & HAWKES

AN IMAGEM COMPANY

DISTRIBUTED BY

HAL•LEONARD®
7777 W. BLUEMOUND RD. P.O. BOX 13819 MILWAUKEE, WI 53213

www.boosey.com
www.halleonard.com

Published by Hendon Music, Inc.
a Boosey & Hawkes company
229 West 28th Street, 11th Floor
New York NY 10001

www.boosey.com

© Copyright 1998 Imagem CV
Administered by Hendon Music, Inc., a Boosey & Hawkes company.
International copyright secured. All rights reserved.

ISMN: 979-0-051-10779-7

Commissioned by Eleanor Eisenmenger and 20th Century Unlimited

for David Leisner and Eugenia Zukerman

COMPOSER'S NOTE

I was an hallucinated fish before. Or, perhaps, that's just a wish. And if it never happened or never will, this music tells how that would be.

—Osvaldo Golijov

EDITOR'S NOTE

When he finished writing *Fish Tale*, Osvaldo Golijov called it a "watercolor", a poetically apt description of its slippery, fluid, evanescent nature. It tells the surrealistic tale of the journey of a fish that begins in the ocean, stops to contemplate the sounds of an African thumb piano, continues on, propelled by the wind, which then becomes a tornado, leading to a waterfall, then is suddenly contained in a little fishbowl, and scurrying on to a long swim in a "rainbow" brook, stops to contemplate the passage of Time, gets caught by a fisherman who fervently promises to return him to the water, dances a bit of samba, considers anew the passage of Time with a sigh, and finally meets the love of his life at the bottom of the sea, dancing a slow waltz to the Brazilian folk music of a "marine music box", which, like an oyster, opens and closes, to music and to silence.

Fish Tale is a kind of "love letter", as the composer wrote to me when he first sent the score. "I wanted everything to be beautiful, even at the expense of some sense". It demands to be played with passion and imagination.

—David Leisner

for David Leisner and Eugenia Zukerman

FISH TALE
for Flute and Guitar

OSVALDO GOLIJOV
Edited by David Leisner

Play as a series of waves with shifting colors

✱ All harmonics sound as written.

979-0-051-10779-7

✻ "My interpretation of the African thumb piano sound is to play the passage sul tasto and very staccato in the left hand, but the player may wish to interpret this in another fashion". – DL

✻✻ The accents should not stop the continuity of these waves.

✱ From measure 67-79, play staccato notes with loud key strokes and almost purely air and color rather than pitch, long notes airy.

OSVALDO GOLIJOV

FISH TALE

FOR FLUTE AND GUITAR

ISBN 978-1-4950-7891-0

HENDON MUSIC

BOOSEY & HAWKES

AN IMAGEM COMPANY

DISTRIBUTED BY

HAL•LEONARD®

7777 W. BLUEMOUND RD. P.O. BOX 13819 MILWAUKEE, WI 53213

www.boosey.com
www.halleonard.com

for David Leisner and Eugenia Zukerman

FISH TALE
for Flute and Guitar

OSVALDO GOLIJOV
Edited by David Leisner

✻ All harmonics sound as written.

✻✻ "My interpretation of the African thumb piano sound is to play the passage sul tasto and very staccato in the left hand, but the player may wish to interpret this in another fashion". – DL

979-0-051-10779-7

poco più mosso

poco rit.

the wind from afar

accel.

sim.

poco riten.
(smorz.)

A tempo (più mosso)

pp sub.   cresc.

poco rit.   a tempo

pp cresc. sempre

accel.   e   cresc.   poco   a   poco

gradually becoming a tornado

sub. meno mosso   accel. e cresc.

p sub.

tornado - waterfall

(cresc. sempre)

✻ The accents should not stop the continuity of these waves.

V.S.

Blank for page turn

Moderato, scorrevole (♩ = c. 54)
Bach: a rainbow brook

piacevole

V.S.

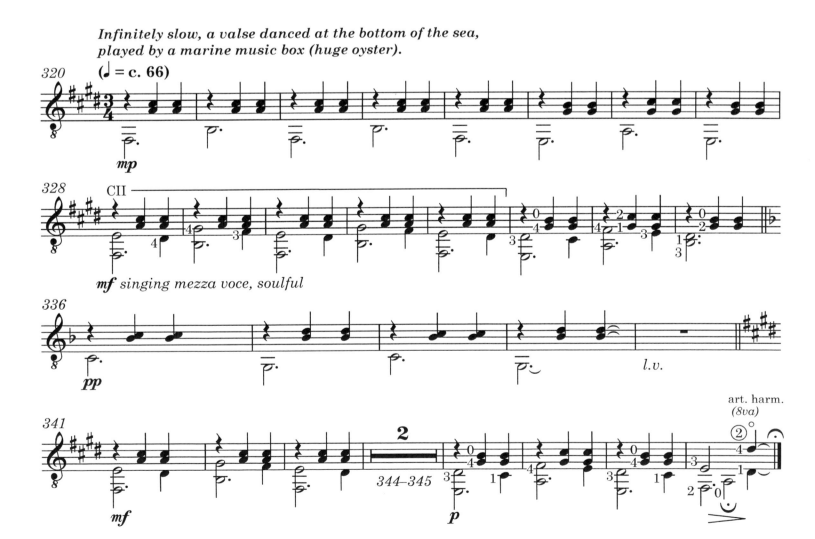

Flute

for David Leisner and Eugenia Zukerman

FISH TALE

for Flute and Guitar

OSVALDO GOLIJOV
Flute Part Edited by Tara O'Connor

979-0-051-10779-7

Flute

* m. 67–97: play staccato notes with loud key strokes and almost purely air and color rather than pitch – long notes airy.

Tempo primo, as in the beginning

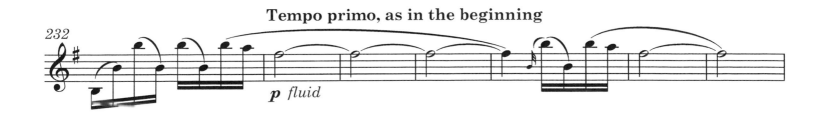

p fluid

hesitant, reminiscing

pp

ppp

♩ = 48

257 *a clock in the water*

port.

port.

p

264 **vivo, rhapsodic**

14

265–278

Flute

Meno mosso

the clock and the sigh

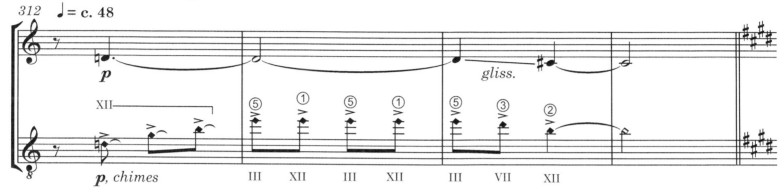

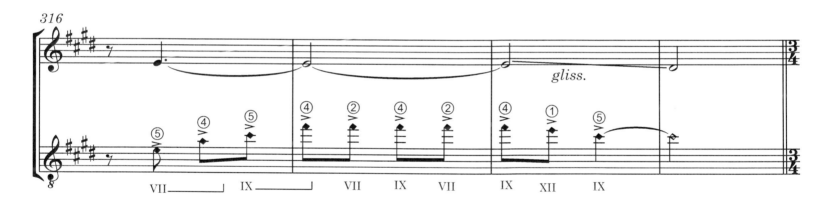

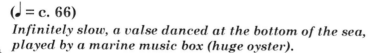

Infinitely slow, a valse danced at the bottom of the sea, played by a marine music box (huge oyster).

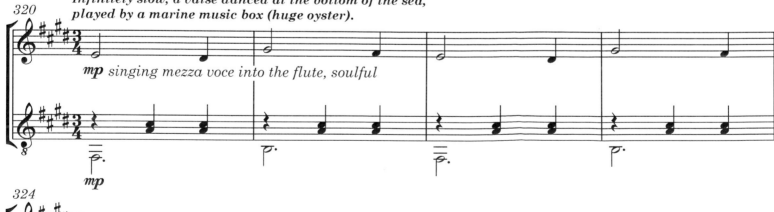

Brookline, May 18, 1998